The Concise Illustrated Book of
Birds of House and Garden

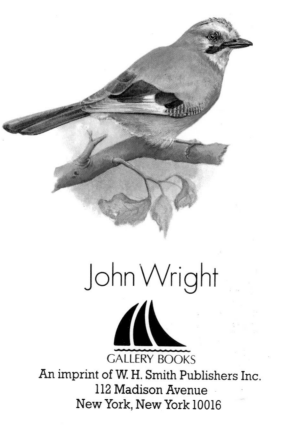

John Wright

GALLERY BOOKS

An imprint of W. H. Smith Publishers Inc.
112 Madison Avenue
New York, New York 10016

First published in the United States of America
by GALLERY BOOKS
An imprint of W.H. Smith Publishers Inc.
112 Madison Avenue
New York, New York 10016

Copyright © 1989 Brian Trodd Publishing
House Limited
Reprinted 1990

ISBN 0-8317-3756-5

Printed in Portugal

Acknowledgments
Front cover photograph of young Swallows
and back cover photograph of a Siskin with
eggs supplied by Images Colour Library,
Leeds.
Eric and David Hosking: 10, 16, 26, 28;
Images Colour Library, Leeds: 11, 15, 24, 25.
The photographs on the remaining pages were
supplied by the Frank Lane Picture Agency
and the following photographers: R. Bird 31;
H.D. Brandl 36, 42; T. Hamblin 19, 30, 32;
P. Heard 22; D. Robinson 34; H. Schrempp
23, 44; R. Tidman 12, 33; J. Watkins 37, 38;
R. Wilmshurst 4, 8, 20, 25, 27, 29, 35, 39, 43;
W. Wisniewski 7; M.B. Withers 18, 21, 41;
D. Zingel 46.
All artworks by Maltings Partnership.

Right: A Whitethroat *(Sylvia Communis)* feeds
its nestlings (see page 16).

CONTENTS

INTRODUCTION

The task of identifying birds may seem daunting but you can easily learn to do it, especially if you start with a selected group of the 30 or so species that may occur in your garden during a year. All bird identification involves a process of elimination based on where and when you see them, plus observation of key features in their appearance, voice or behaviour.

First, remember that few birds occur everywhere. Because they have particular needs for food or nest sites, most are confined to particular types of habitat such as woodland, open fields and rivers. Within a habitat, different species may have particular preferences. Thus Chiffchaffs breed in mature woodland, but the very similar Willow Warbler often occurs in young woods and scrub. So where you see a bird is an important clue to its identity.

This book groups together birds which occur in gardens though, as you will see from the habitat descriptions, they do use other sites as well. In general, garden birds are those which naturally occur in scrub and woodland edges, because these are the kinds of conditions created artificially in gardens by ornamental trees and shrubs, lawns and flowerbeds.

Second, remember that the national distribution of birds varies for climatic and geographical reasons. Many birds are common in the gardens of one region, but are rarities indeed elsewhere.

Third, the time of year is often important in identifying birds. Some will be present only in winter, others only in summer. With a bit of experience you will come to know where to expect to see birds, and when, so that the list of possibilities will be much reduced.

Finally, consider any unknown bird's physical appearance. At first it seems an impossible problem to remember all the complicated details of plumage of a bird such as a Goldfinch, but in fact you do not need to remember everything. The general impression is important—overall colour or some very conspicuous marking, such as bright yellow flashes in the wings, will often narrow the choice. Note the bird's head pattern, because this is so distinctive in most cases that it will give you all the guidance you need without confusing you with too much to remember. Has it a cap like a Marsh Tit or facial stripes like a Redwing, for instance? If you have enough time, look for the number and colour of bars in the wings, and only then for other marks and coloration. Always keep in mind that the markings of birds may differ with their sexes, and that young birds may have quite different plumage from that of the adults—a good example of this is the young Blackbird which is quite speckled on its light underparts. Size is important too. This is not difficult to judge if you use familiar comparisons, such as the Blue Tit, House Sparrow and Pigeon.

Once you start observing birds, you will realize that each species carries itself differently—tits are acrobatic in foliage, Blackbirds hop, Pied Wagtails always run and wag their tails, Robins hold themselves upright, but Dunnocks creep mousily. Is the bird's flight steady and direct like a Starling's or bouncing like a Linnet's? When you learn a bird's way of moving (its 'jizz'), then you will often be able to identify it even as a silhouette against the light.

The greatest challenge of all, when you can identify your garden birds by sight, is to try to learn their songs and calls. They are frustratingly difficult to write down but remarkably distinctive in life. Outside the garden, especially in woods and hedges, you will hear many more birds than you see and it is hugely rewarding to be able to recognize the return of the Waxwing in winter or the arrival of Swallows in summer simply from a soft call in the tree tops or the night sky.

Habitat: Towns and villages, isolated houses, bridges and cliffs both inland and at the coast.

Distribution: Throughout the British Isles but sparse in northern Scotland and most common in the farmed lowlands of England and Wales.

Seasons: A summer migrant, most birds arriving in April and leaving in October, though birds on passage through Britain from the north may be seen until December.

Description: *Size* 13cm (5in). The House Martin is the only bird of its kind to have a white rump: Swallows lack the white rump and have tail streamers and red faces; Swifts are bigger and dark all over. Both sexes look the same and young birds are slightly browner than their parents.

Voice: A clear 'tchirrip', often heard as a storm of sound when many birds are calling at once. The note changes to a higher-pitched nervous 'tseep' when a predator such as a bird of prey is sighted.

Food: Insects caught on the wing.

Behaviour: When prospecting for nest sites, the birds will hang twittering on the house wall beneath the eaves. From late summer, parties gather on telegraph wires or roofs, sometimes with smaller numbers of Swallows.

Breeding: The mud nest is constructed in the angle of wall and eaves. Birds may breed alone or in colonies, sometimes several dozen strong. The first nests are often taken over by House Sparrows, forcing the martins to build afresh. Four or five eggs are laid and there can be two or three broods in the nesting season.

SWALLOW

Hirundo rustica

Habitat: Farmland and heaths, areas with open water or reedbeds. Requires access to buildings or other covered structures for nesting.

Distribution: Throughout Britain and Ireland. It is a summer visitor to the U.S.A. and western Canada where it is called Barn Swallow.

Seasons: A summer visitor, the first-comers arriving in late March and stragglers still migrating south in early winter.

Description: *Size* 16–22cm (6–8½in), the difference reflecting the extra length of the male's tail streamers. Note that these streamers make the tails of both sexes seem much more deeply forked than those of House Martins and Swifts, but this is not so with young birds. At all ages Swallows have red and blue faces, whereas House Martins have white cheeks and throats; Swallows are uniformly dark above but House Martins have white rumps.

Voice: A high 'tswit', often repeated several times rapidly. Song given in flight or from a perch is a pleasing mix of twitters and warbling.

Food: Insects caught in flight over open land or over water.

Behaviour: Swallows tend to fly lower than House Martins and Swifts, often cruising less than a metre (three feet) off the ground. Like martins they perch on wires and sometimes in trees. Large groups gather in autumn prior to migration.

Breeding: The cup-shaped nest is always placed under cover of a roof, bridge or other structure and is supported on a beam, ledge or shelf, the birds flying in and out through an opening. There can be up to three broods of 4–6 young.

Corvus monedula

Habitat: Mature woodland, parks and farmland with trees, sea cliffs and quarries. Where suitable nest sites are accessible, also in towns and villages; the birds fly out to farmland to feed.

Distribution: Throughout the British Isles but very sparse or absent in the north and west of Scotland. Perhaps most abundant where there is plentiful pasture on which to feed. It is a rare visitor to the north-east regions of the U.S.A.

Seasons: The resident British population is supplemented in winter by immigrants from continental Europe.

Description: *Size* 33cm (13in). Much bigger than a Blackbird. Adults have a light grey nape but juveniles are all black. Rooks, which may occasionally visit gardens in rural areas, are larger (45cm: 17¾in), and the adults have a white patch at the base of the beak and shaggy trousers which cover the upper legs. Jackdaws have bare legs.

Voice: A cheerful, sharp 'chak' or 'jack' and a shrill 'keeaw'. Often several birds will call at once, making a sudden clatter of noise.

Food: Many kinds of insects, worms, slugs, grain and berries picked from the ground, as well as caterpillars taken from the foliage of trees. Jackdaws will also take the eggs and nestlings of other birds.

Behaviour: Gregarious, sometimes in parties dozens or even hundreds strong and often seen flying and feeding with rooks. It tends to be bold and inquisitive.

Breeding: The untidy stick nest is placed in a cavity in a tree or rock crevice, or down a chimney. Four or six eggs are laid and a single brood is reared in each year.

MAGPIE

Pica pica

Habitat: Woodland edges, scrub, farmland especially pasture with livestock, hedges, parks and gardens.

Distribution: England, Wales and Ireland, lowland Scotland: patchily in the Highlands. Also found in parts of California.

Seasons: Resident.

Description: *Size* 46cm (18in) including the long tail. Unmistakable, as the only other black and white garden bird is the Pied Wagtail, which is very much smaller (18cm: 7in). At close range much of the black plumage has an iridescent green and blue hue. Young birds are short-tailed versions of their parents.

Voice: A coarse rattling 'chak-achak-achaka' unlike any other bird.

Food: Almost anything which is abundant or easily found, including insects and worms, berries and fruit, grain, small mammals, eggs and nestlings, and carrion.

Behaviour: Though much persecuted for its predation of game bird eggs, the Magpie is common and widespread in most lowland areas. Its apparent boldness reflects a nice ability to judge danger from people, and egg hunting visits to gardens are often carried out in the early morning before there is much human activity. Sometimes occurs in large, noisy groups at roost sites and at the start of the nesting season.

Breeding: A large nest is built, often fairly low in scrub or saplings, and roofed with thorny twigs for protection against other nest predators especially crows. There are 5–7 eggs and one brood in the season.

Sylvia atricapilla

Habitat: Broadleaved woodlands with abundant undergrowth of bushes or brambles. Large gardens with trees and plenty of shrubs.

Distribution: All England and Wales, lowland Scotland, central and eastern Ireland.

Seasons: A summer visitor arriving in April and leaving by September. However, in the south migrants may be seen in March and October. A small number overwinter in southern England and eastern Ireland.

Description: *Size* 14cm (5½in). Has a black crown and can be confused with a Marsh Tit or Willow Tit, but has grey cheeks whereas theirs are white. They also have a small black bib under the chin, which the Blackcap lacks. The female is a warmer brown than the male and has a brown crown. Young birds are dull versions of their parents. All Blackcaps have a very slender appearance.

Voice: A delightful rich warble, usually coming from within dense shrubbery. The song is easily confused with that of the garden warbler. Also a hard 'tacc . . . tacc' note, like a tongue-click.

Food: Insects picked from the foliage, and berries in autumn.

Behaviour: Often skulking and hard to see as it moves about inside foliage, never coming to the ground. Even when in full song, males are quick to slip back into cover when disturbed.

Breeding: The cup-shaped nest is concealed in dense hedges or shrubs, brambles, ivy or other evergreen cover. Four or five eggs are laid and there may be two broods.

CHIFFCHAFF

Phylloscopus collybita

Habitat: Mature woodland with tall trees and rough undergrowth is the favourite habitat, but Chiffchaffs also sometimes breed in hedges with trees. They are most likely to be seen in gardens when on migration, seeking food in shrubs, rose bushes and hedges.

Distribution: Throughout the lowlands of the British Isles.

Seasons: A summer visitor, one of the first to arrive and the last to leave, with birds present in the south from early March to October. Small numbers overwinter in some areas of south-west England.

Description: *Size* 11cm (4¼in). A good deal smaller than a House Sparrow and noticeably slender, the Chiffchaff appears a rather nondescript greeny-grey little bird. A closer look reveals paler, yellowish underparts and a light stripe extending over the eye. Very similar in appearance to the Willow Warbler, the legs are usually dark grey whereas those of Willow Warblers are pink. But even experienced birdwatchers find the two species hard to separate and often refer to both as 'willow-chiffs'!

Voice: A sure means of identification, the bird sings its own name 'chiff-chaff . . . chiff-chaff' from the crowns of trees. The call is a loud 'hweet'.

Food: Insects from trees and shrubs.

Behaviour: Slips through the foliage with agility, appearing fidgety as it flicks its wings and tail repeatedly. Rarely comes to the ground to feed.

Breeding: The domed nest is concealed in a tangle of herbage and shrubs, usually within 60cm (2ft) of the ground. Six eggs are laid and two broods may be reared.

Sylvia borin

Habitat: Mainly broadleaved woodland with a dense understorey of shrubs and brambles; also young plantations of both broadleaves and conifers giving similar shrubby cover, provided there are also some older trees; occasionally in gardens or adjoining suitable woodland.

Distribution: Widespread in England and Wales and southern Scotland. Very scattered in northern Scotland and is also extremely rare in Ireland.

Seasons: Summer visitor present in mid-April to September.

Description: *Size* 14cm (5½in). A bird identifiable by its lack of obvious distinguishing characteristics! The impression is of a greeny-buff bird, slightly paler below, with a large eye and neatly rounded head. May be confused with the Chiffchaff and Willow Warbler but they have more obvious pale eyestripes, rather flattened crowns and a stronger yellow-green coloration.

Voice: The song is very similar to that of a Blackcap, a melodious warbling often delivered from within cover, but is usually sustained while Blackcaps tend to break their song up into shorter phrases. Alarm calls are like those of Blackcap but softer.

Food: Insects picked from foliage, and berries in autumn.

Behaviour: A very discreet bird usually seen only briefly before it retreats back into cover. Normally uses trees or saplings as song posts but often found in sites with fewer trees than Blackcap.

Breeding: The nest is usually placed below 1m (3ft 3in) from the ground or on the ground itself, well hidden in the dense cover of low brambles, briars or shrubs or other thick undergrowth.

GOLDCREST

Regulus regulus

Habitat: In Britain, primarily evergreen conifer woodland, but also found in parks, churchyards and gardens where there are stands of yews or ornamental conifers. Much less common in broadleaved woodlands except in Ireland, where it can be abundant.

Distribution: Throughout Britain and Ireland.

Seasons: The resident population is joined by birds from continental Europe in winter.

Description: *Size* 9cm (3½in). The smallest garden bird, Goldcrests really do seem tiny. The overall impression is of a dullish green bird but note the darker wings with a clear white wing bar, the black stripe along the crown and the central gold stripe which is quite easy to see as the bird swings acrobatically in the foliage. Young birds lack the head pattern.

Voice: A high-pitched, repeated 'zee-zee-zee' which can be confused with a Coal Tit (see Marsh Tit). The song is a repeated double note 'zeeda' ending with a squeaky flourish – like a distant, squeaking cartwheel.

Food: Small insects and spiders.

Behaviour: Feeds at all heights from just above ground level to the tops of trees, often in family parties or, in winter, mixed with titmice. Tends to ignore humans so it can be watched at close range.

Breeding: The nest is a ball of moss and spiders' web suspended by 'handles' near the end of a horizontal branch, or in ivy. There may be seven or eight eggs and two broods of young.

Habitat: Woodland edges and forest glades where the bird can find nest sites in trees and good feeding opportunities in the open spaces. Also orchards, hedges with trees, old churchyards and parks. Occurs in gardens with large trees around lawns.

Distribution: Throughout the British Isles.

Seasons: A summer visitor which arrives in late April and departs in September.

Description: *Size* 14cm (5½in), about the same as a sparrow but looks larger because of its characteristic way of perching bolt upright. In some lights, Spotted Flycatchers can appear almost uniformly grey, but there is a faint speckling on the forehead and, more noticeably, on the throat and chest. Young birds have a rather scaly appearance, the feathers of the head, back and breast having dark edges to white centres.

Voice: The song consists of half a dozen thin, squeaky notes, well separated. It is easy to miss!

Food: Insects mostly caught in flight.

Behaviour: The very distinctive hunting technique is a very good means of identification. A Spotted Flycatcher will perch in the open, choosing a protruding branch and sitting very upright to watch for passing insects; then it will fly out, capture its prey and return to the same perch or another nearby. Note that several garden birds 'fly catch' occasionally but none so skilfully as this species.

Breeding: The nest is often in a tree cavity or behind climbing plants on a wall. Open-fronted nestboxes are readily used. There may be two broods of 4–5 young.

WHITETHROAT

Sylvia communis

Habitat: Scrub or heaths, commons, downs and wasteland, hedgerows, woodland edges. In gardens when on migration.

Distribution: Throughout the British Isles except Orkney and Shetland.

Seasons: Summer visitor present mid-April to September.

Description: *Size* 14cm (5½in). The contrast between the grey head, brown back and very pale underparts is quite striking. Indeed, the name draws attention to the very obvious white throat. Note also the rather peaked crown shape. Confusion is possible with the Lesser Whitethroat which also uses scrub habitats but which is greyer above and has a very dark grey cheek patch like a highway-man's mask.

Voice: The song is a short vigorous mix of chattering and scratchy notes – bags of enthusiasm but not much talent. Has a 'tac . . . tac' call like that of a Blackcap, a scolding 'tcharr' and a quiet 'wheet-wheet . . . wit-wit-wit'. The Lesser Whitethroat's song is quite different – a rapid single-note rattle.

Food: Insects plus berries in autumn.

Behaviour: The male is very obvious in spring because his song is delivered from a conspicuous perch on a bush or hedge, or in a dancing song flight – rising from the top of a bush and then fluttering down to the same or another perch. Otherwise, more often heard than seen as the bird calls or scolds from cover.

Breeding: Up to 60cm (2ft) off the ground, the nests are concealed in cover of shrubs or tall herbage. There may be two broods of 4–5 eggs.

Phylloscopus trochilus

Habitat: All kinds of woodland provided there are patches of young tree growth or scrub and rough herbage or rank grass. Visits gardens mainly when on migration.

Distribution: Throughout the British Isles but the Willow Warbler does not breed in Shetland.

Seasons: Summer visitor, some seen in March but most arriving in April. The Willow Warbler departs from September to November.

Description: *Size* 11cm (4¼in). Almost identical to the Chiffchaff but tends to be slightly yellower, though experience of both birds is needed before attempting to identify in this way. Legs tend to be flesh coloured whereas Chiffchaff's legs are dark grey but this is often not easy to see. The main distinguishing feature is the voice.

Voice: The song is a pleasing ripple of notes, first rising in pitch and then cascading away to a neat flourish, repeated again and again after a few seconds pause. One of the commonest sounds in springtime woods and scrub, it is completely different from the Chiffchaff's eponymous song. The call is a plaintive two notes.

Food: Insects gathered from foliage.

Behaviour: Restless, usually seen busily feeding in the treetops or in scrubby growth down nearly to ground level. Hovers to pick food from leaves and sometimes captures insects in flight, like a Flycatcher. When in gardens, usually seen feeding in rose bushes or shrubs, not staying long.

Breeding: The nests are domed and built on the ground in rough herbage or grass. There are 6–7 eggs and two broods may be produced in a year.

BLACKBIRD

Turdus merula

Habitat: Woodland, farm hedges, parks and gardens where there are trees to sing from, bushes for nesting, and soft ground for feeding.

Distribution: Throughout Britain and Ireland except on the uplands.

Seasons: Resident all year except in some northern districts where the birds move away in winter.

Description: *Size* 24–27cm (9½–10½in). Males are the only medium-sized all-black birds, much smaller than Jackdaws or Rooks. Adult males have bright orange beaks. The hens are mid-brown with slight speckling on the throat, and the young birds are quite speckled on their light under-parts, but duller than thrushes.

Voice: A beautifully rich fluting song. Both sexes have a hysterical chinking alarm call and will scold predators, or settle to roost, with a repeated 'tuc . . . tuc'.

Food: Berries and soft fruit, worms, small snails, insects and kitchen scraps.

Behaviour: Feeds on the ground, hopping in the open and under shrubs and hedges where it can be heard noisily scrabbling amongst the dead leaves. Usually flies low, alternately flapping and gliding. Raises and fans the tail on landing. Males have 'hopping races' in spring when competing with each other for territory.

Breeding: The nest is a cup of grasses and rootlets securely placed in forking branches of a bush, usually low down and sometimes even on the ground; occasionally in buildings. Often one of the earliest breeders, with eggs in early March. There are 3–5 bluish eggs, heavily mottled with pinky-brown. Three or more broods may be raised in a season.

Turdus pilaris

Habitat: Mostly open farmland including grazed pasture, ploughed fields and hedges with berries. Sometimes in open woodlands. Fieldfares visit gardens occasionally, mostly when snow or frost make feeding on farmland difficult.

Distribution: Almost all of the British Isles in winter but birds move about in response to weather conditions and may be locally abundant one day and then totally absent. Some-

times occurs in Alaska, east Canada and the north-east of the U.S.A.

Seasons: Winter visitor, the first arrivals appearing in September, but most do not reach us until October. Departure is in March and April. A few pairs breed in woodland margins or scrub in upland areas of northern England and Scotland.

Description: *Size* 25cm (10in). A large, boldly marked thrush, bigger than a Blackbird. The combination of grey head and rump, black tail, brown wings and orangey-speckled breast is quite unmistakable. Both sexes are similar.

Voice: A loud confident chattering 'chak-chak-chak'. Flocks often very vocal when feeding and in flight.

Food: Berries and insects. Stands of hawthorn and rowan trees are much favoured, as are fallen apples, and in gardens the birds may visit shrubs such as Pyracantha and Cotoneaster.

Behaviour: Fieldfares are hard to miss because of their large size, flocking habits and loud calls. They often occur in mixed flocks with Redwings, and may be found feeding in trees and shrubs or on the ground. In gardens, birds may occur singly and be shy of human activity, sometimes flying off even at movement at a window.

MISTLE THRUSH

Turdus viscivorus

Habitat: Grassland with trees on farms, playing fields, parks and larger gardens.

Distribution: Throughout British Isles but not Orkney or Shetland.

Seasons: Resident, plus some migrants from the continent in winter.

Description: *Size* 26cm (10in). Bigger than a Song Thrush and with more bulk, giving the impression of being strongly built. Both sexes are similar and, compared with the Song Thrush, have larger, better defined spots extending further down onto the belly. Overall the birds also look paler – almost grey in some lights. Young birds have pale speckling on the head and back.

Voice: A hard 'tuc-tuc-tuc' and a loud clatter like a wooden rattle. The song is powerful, varied as a Blackbird's but more rapidly delivered and with a less mellow tone. Song begins in very early spring.

Food: Insects and worms collected from short grassland, plus some berries and fruit.

Behaviour: Usually seen on grasslands such as playing fields, hopping briefly and pausing to look for food. It has a more upright stance than a Song Thrush. Often seen singly or in pairs, though larger parties are seen in late summer. It sings from the topmost bough of a chosen tree, and is bold in defence of its nest, launching vigorous attacks on Magpies or other predators, accompanied by rattling alarm calls.

Breeding: The cup-shaped nest is placed in a tree fork – yews and apple trees seem to be preferred if available. 3–5 eggs are laid and there are normally two broods in a year.

Phoenicurus phoenicurus

Habitat: Mature broadleaved woodland and ancient pinewoods with open glades or little ground cover. Hedges and parkland with old trees. Gardens close to these habitats.

Distribution: Largely south-west England, the Pennines and north-west Wales, western Scotland. Scarce in lowland areas. Very rare in Ireland.

Seasons: The Redstart is a summer visitor, and is present April to September.

Description: *Size* 14cm (5½in). The most obvious feature is the red tail, which is constantly shivered. The breeding male is quite exotically handsome with red breast, black face, white forehead and bluish upperparts. Females are a modest buff above and pale below while young birds have scaly-looking mottled brown backs and spotted breasts, but all share the red tail. Confusion is possible with the Black Redstart – a much darker bird which breeds at a handful of city or industrial sites in England where some birds also overwinter.

Voice: The song resembles a Robin's, but quickly tails off. However, the birds have a combined plaintive whistle and ticking noise which is a very distinctive 'hweet, tuc-tuc'.

Food: Insects and some berries.

Behaviour: Feeds on ground and in foliage. Often perches in low branches at the bottom of a tree's canopy. Restless, flitting down to ground and up, or between trees. The constantly shivering tail is an excellent identification feature when the bird is only seen in silhouette.

Breeding: Nests in cavities, usually in a tree but sometimes in walls or in quarries. Five to seven eggs are laid and there are sometimes two broods.

REDWING

Turdus iliacus

Habitat: Woodland, scrub and hedges with berries. Pasture and ploughed fields. Sometimes in gardens with berry-bearing trees and shrubs.

Seasons: A winter visitor arriving in September and leaving by April. A very few remain to breed.

Distribution: All Britain and Ireland, but the birds move around as local food supplies are exhausted, and in response to snow or prolonged frost.

Description: *Size* 21cm (8in), slightly smaller than a Blackbird. The name comes from a band of red along the front edge of the underwing which is very obvious when in flight. The colour also spreads to the upper flanks, forming a red streak below the edge of the wing when the bird is at rest. Note that Song Thrushes have a much paler, buff colouring in the same place. At close range, the white stripes through the eye and below the cheek are quite striking and distinct from the fainter markings on Song Thrushes.

Voice: Listen out on calm nights in autumn for Redwings migrating overhead – their drawn out 'see-ip' flight calls are quite often heard. When feeding, birds chatter 'chittuk'.

Food: Worms and insects collected from grass and ploughed land. Berries gathered from rowan, holly, hawthorn and, sometimes, garden shrubs.

Behaviour: Normally in flocks, often together with Fieldfares.

Breeding: A very few pairs nest in the Scottish Highlands, sometimes in gardens.

Erithacus rubecula

Habitat: All woodland, though more abundant in broadleaved than conifer woods. Farm hedges, parks and most gardens, especially where there is cultivated ground.

Distribution: Throughout Britain and Ireland.

Seasons: Mostly resident, though some British birds winter in south-west Europe and others come to Britain in winter from the Continent.

Distribution: 14cm (5½in). Doubt-

less the best known bird in the British Isles, though many people do not recognize young robins which have 'scaly' backs and underparts, their feathers having pale centres and dark margins. Gradually the back darkens and the breast becomes red.

Voice: A ticking call note and a gentle song of distinct notes with a rather melancholy quality. Robins sing not only in spring but also in autumn, when establishing winter territories.

Food: Small insects and worms picked mainly from bare soil, plus some seeds and berries. A regular visitor to birdtables.

Breeding: The nest is built in a cavity on or near the ground. The classic site is an old kettle wedged in a hedge bottom and open-fronted nestboxes are often used. There are about six eggs and up to three broods may be reared in a single season.

THE AMERICAN ROBIN (*Turdus migratorius*), illustrated right, is the North American equivalent of the European Blackbird and is a rare visitor to Western Europe. Voice and behaviour resemble the Blackbird and juveniles have spotted breasts.

The American Robin (*Turdus Migratorius*)

SONG THRUSH

Turdus philomelos

Habitat: Woodland, scrub, farm hedges, parks and many gardens where there are lawns for feeding and large shrubs or hedges for nesting.

Distribution: Throughout Britain and Ireland but not Shetland.

Seasons: Present all year but some British birds winter in south-west Europe, while some from northern Europe winter in the British Isles and others pass through on their way further south.

Description: *Size* 23cm (9in), seeming slightly smaller than the Blackbird because the tail is shorter. Warmer brown than the Mistle Thrush with more dense streaking on the upper breast and an unmarked belly. The underwing shows a pale orangey-fawn patch when the bird is in flight, much less brilliant than the colour on a Redwing. Young Song Thrushes have faint pale streaky marks on the crown and back.

Voice: A pleasing song, less richly toned than the Blackbird's and consisting of short phrases, each often being sung twice. A common phrase in most songs can be rendered as 'pretty joey, pretty joey'.

Food: Largely insects, worms, slugs and snails. Much less soft fruit and berries than Blackbirds.

Behaviour: When feeding, hops or runs briefly and then pauses, head cocked as though listening, but actually eyeing for tell-tale movements of worms or other prey. Carries snails to a handy stone to hammer them open. It does not flock.

Breeding: The nest is quite often built very low down in dense evergreen or shrub cover but can be well up in trees. There are four eggs and there can be more than two broods.

Parus caeruleus

Habitat: Broadleaved and, less commonly, coniferous woodlands, hedges with trees, parks and gardens with trees and shrubs.

Distribution: Throughout Britain and Ireland except the northern and western Isles.

Seasons: Resident, with some winter immigration in some years.

Description: *Size* 11cm (4¼in), substantially smaller than a Great Tit. Both sexes look the same though the colours tend to be brightest in spring. Young birds are 'washed out' versions of the adults with a greenish-yellow cast to the whole plumage and with a brownish crown rather than blue.

Voice: A quick, high pitched 'tsee-tsee-tsee-tsit' and a harsher, scolding 'churrr'. The song is a high 'tsee-tsee-tsee-turrr', the last sound becoming a trill.

Food: Mainly insects picked from foliage and twigs, but also seeds, berries and fruit.

Behaviour: Very agile, swinging upside-down in the treetops or working through low-growing shrubs in search of food. Sometimes comes to the ground to feed. A regular visitor to nutbags and, in some places, removes milk bottle tops to drink cream. Noisy, often giving its scolding alarm when humans approach. Occurs in flocks with other tits in winter.

Breeding: Nests in small holes and cavities, normally in trees but also walls. Takes readily to nestboxes with a 2.5cm (1in) diameter entrance – too small to permit use by larger birds. There can be up to 16 eggs, though 10 to 12 is more normal, and in most years only one brood is reared.

GREAT TIT

Parus major

Habitat: Broadleaved woods and, less abundantly, conifers, scrub, farm hedges with trees, parks and gardens.
Distribution: Throughout Britain and Ireland except the northern and western Isles.
Seasons: Resident all year.
Description: *Size* 14cm (5½in), about sparrow-size. The dark blue head marking runs completely round under the white cheek and continues all down the centre of the bird's underparts. This centre stripe is usually much broader in males than females. Young birds are much duller than the adults, their heads tending to be greeny-brown and off-yellow rather than navy blue and white, but the overall pattern of markings is the same.
Voice: The usual call is a clear 'pink pink' very similar to that of a Chaffinch. There is also a scolding 'chi-chi-chi' not unlike that of a Blue Tit but usually more deeply pitched. The song is a loud, cheerful disyllabic 'tee-cher . . . tee-cher' rather like sawing. Take care not to confuse it with the more musical song of the Chiffchaff.
Food: Insects mainly gathered in the foliage of trees and shrubs or from bark. Berries, fruits and seeds, often gathered from the ground.
Behaviour: Almost as acrobatic as the Blue Tit but feeds more often on the ground. Visits nutbags and bird-tables. In winter may flock with other titmice in woodland.
Breeding: Nests in holes usually in trees and will occupy nestboxes with an entry of 3cm (1¼in) diameter or more. Up to 12 eggs are laid and there is usually only a single brood.

Aegithalos caudatus

Habitat: Woodland edges and, more frequently, scrub, thick hedgerows, coppice and bramble thickets.

Distribution: England, Wales, Ireland and most of Scotland but absent from the northern and western Isles.

Seasons: Resident. Numbers are often reduced by hard winters.

Description: *Size* 14cm (5½in) including the long tail. The bill and body are tiny and the bird is virtually impossible to misidentify, with its pleasing pattern of pink, white and black plumage. Male and female are similar but young birds have slightly shorter tails and dark cheeks.

Voice: A little puttering 'tupp . . . tupp' is the most usual call, seeming not loud but with a carrying quality. There is also a weak, persistent 'zee-zee-zee' and a rippling 'tsirrup' call.

Food: Mainly small insects.

Behaviour: In autumn and winter Long-tailed Tits are rather conspicuous birds, moving about in parties of a dozen or so and keeping contact by constant calls as they flit busily between bushes and trees in a search for insects. They regularly pass through gardens with enough trees or shrubs to attract them, but normally stay only a few minutes in one place. When nesting, the birds become more secretive and can be easily overlooked.

Breeding: An oval ball of moss, cobwebs and hair, lined with up to 2000 feathers, is placed in shrubs, creepers or against the trunk of a tree. A single brood of 7–12 young may be reared in a nesting season.

MARSH TIT

Parus palustris

Habitat: Despite the name, this is not a marshland bird but largely confined to broadleaved woodlands. Visits gardens near such woods.

Distribution: England and Wales, becoming scarcer in the north. A few pairs breed in south Scotland. Absent from Ireland.

Seasons: Resident.

Description: *Size* 12cm (4¾in). The plumage is a neat pattern of brown, white and black. Both adults and young birds have a similar appearance. Confusion is possible with two other kinds of tits. The Willow Tit – which does occur in marshy woodlands – is very similar but has a pale patch on the wing. It rarely visits gardens. The Coal Tit has a more olive-coloured back, twin white wingbars and a large white patch on the back of the head. It is much associated with conifer trees and may visit gardens which contain them.

Voice: A loud 'pitchew', a nasal 'tchair' and a scolding alarm 'chicka-dee-dee-dee' – hence the American name Chickadee for a closely related bird.

Food: Insects, berries and seeds of trees and shrubs.

Behaviour: It is much less common than Blue or Great Tits and much shyer, but sometimes visits nutbags and birdtables. Largely a bird of trees and shrubs, but sometimes feeds on the ground. In winter, joins with other tits in foraging flocks.

Breeding: Nests in holes or cracks in trees or stumps from near ground level to high up. Rarely uses nestboxes. There are 6–8 eggs and only one brood.

Habitat: Beech woods are preferred, but Bramblings also feed on tilled farmland and at garden birdtables.

Distribution: Varies greatly from year to year but can be found in winter throughout England and Wales, except the south-west, and sparsely in eastern Ireland. Occurs occasionally in Alaska, Canada and western states of the U.S.A.

Seasons: A winter visitor, arriving in October in variable numbers depending on the availability of food in continental Europe, and sometimes still present in May. A very few pairs occasionally breed in birch and conifer woods in Scotland.

Description: *Size* 15cm (6in) the same as the Chaffinch, to which it is closely related. The Brambling's combination of orange and black markings is not found in any other garden visitor. The females are rather paler than the males, the breast tending to a warm buff colour. In summer, the male has a striking black head and nape. When flying, both sexes show white rumps, a feature shared only with the rather portly-looking Bullfinch which, however, never occurs in large flocks.

Voice: A rather harsh 'tsweek' and, in spring, a drawn out 'tzwee' very like that of a male Greenfinch.

Food: Tree seeds especially beech-mast, and other seeds and berries.

Behaviour: In winter it occurs in flocks which may be very large, feeding on the ground in woodland and flying up into the trees if disturbed. When natural food is in short supply, some exceptionally bold individuals may visit birdtables.

BULLFINCH

Pyrrhula pyrrhula

Habitat: Broadleaved woodland, young conifer plantations, orchards, scrub, hedges and gardens. Does not visit birdtables but appreciates the buds of fruit trees, gooseberry and currant bushes!

Distribution: Found throughout Britain and Ireland except on the highest ground and on some offshore islands. Occasionally occurs in Alaska.

Seasons: Resident all year.

Description: *Size* 15cm (6in). The brilliant pinky-red cheeks, breast and belly of the cock Bullfinch are unmistakable. The female is paler, with buff-pink underparts but shares with the male the black crown, stout black beak and generally portly appearance. Young birds lack the black crown and are a somewhat uniform brown above and below but, like their parents, have black wings with a bold white stripe. In flight, Bullfinches show a white rump contrasting with a black tail.

Voice: A soft, plangent piping 'deeu', repeated at intervals.

Food: Seeds such as ash keys, berries, buds of many kinds of trees and shrubs, and insects. Damage to fruit trees is most likely when there has been a poor crop of wild tree seeds and berries.

Behaviour: Often seen in pairs or small parties. Rarely found in the open. When flushed, the birds will fly from one patch of bushes to the next but often sit up where they can be seen and watched without difficulty.

Breeding: The nest is concealed in thick cover, often in evergreens. Four to six eggs are laid and two broods may be reared.

Fringilla coelebs

Habitat: Chaffinches are the commonest woodland birds in most of the British Isles and also nest in trees, in hedges and gardens. During autumn and winter, they often feed in ploughed fields and in gardens.

Distribution: Throughout the British Isles, except Shetland.

Seasons: Resident all year, with a winter influx of birds from northern Europe which return to the Continent by April.

Description: *Size* 15cm (6in). The male's pastel blue crown and pink-chestnut underparts are distinctive. Females and young birds tend to give a general impression of rather drab green colouring, though a close look shows that this is mainly on the back as the head and underparts are a soft grey-beige. Both adults and juveniles are the only garden birds with twin white bars on each wing.

Voice: A loud 'pink-pink' easily confused with the call of the Great Tit. The male's song is a cheerful, hurried 'chip-chip-chip-chewy-chewy-tissy-chewy-oo', with a few seconds pause before each repetition.

Food: Plant and tree seeds when adult. However, the young are fed on insects, especially caterpillars.

Behaviour: Chaffinches are easily seen as they tend to perch on the outsides of trees and often feed on open ground. In the countryside, the birds form flocks in winter, frequently composed of a single sex. Usually gardens are visited by one or two birds only.

Breeding: A neat nest, camouflaged with mosses and lichens, is built in the fork of a fairly low branch and a single brood of four or five young is reared.

GOLDFINCH

Carduelis carduelis

Habitat: Open areas such as wasteland with abundant seeding plants. Tall bushes or trees are needed for nesting and the birds will commute between suitable feeding and nesting areas. Nests in large gardens and, much more often, in orchards.

Distribution: Common in southern England, Wales and Ireland: less abundant in northern England and lowland Scotland.

Seasons: Most migrate south in winter, returning in April, and summer numbers fluctuate being highest in warm, dry years.

Description: *Size* 12cm (4¾in). The broad yellow bar shows up brilliantly on the black wing whether the bird is perched or in flight. Both adults have a striking scarlet face and black crowns. Young birds have buff heads and bodies with fainter yellow wingbars.

Voice: Most often a liquid twittering 'swift-witt-witt-witt' often heard from birds in flight. The male song has a similar liquid tone.

Food: Seeds of weeds such as dandelions, knapweed, teasels and thistles.

Behaviour: Often in twittering family parties or small flocks, flying low with the rather bounding flight characteristic of finches, gathering to feed acrobatically on the seed heads of weeds, or to pick seeds from the ground.

Breeding: Frequently several pairs nest close to each other, constructing their nests in the forks of slender branches, where they sway in the wind. Five or six eggs are laid and there can be up to three broods.

GREENFINCH

Carduelis chloris

Habitat: A bird of woodland edges, patches of scrub, hedges with trees, parks and gardens. As a breeding bird it requires trees or tall shrubs but in winter many visit small gardens.

Distribution: Ireland and Britain except north-west Scotland.

Seasons: Present all year round but some breeding birds migrate south, and some continental birds winter in the British Isles.

Description: *Size* 15cm (6in). This

bird is solidly-built with a low-crowned, thick-necked appearance. Often seems more yellow than green, as the male has bright yellow underparts and yellow patches in the wings and tail which show up vividly in flight. Females are much duller, yellowy-buff coloured birds, and juveniles are buff with speckled underparts, but all share the yellow wing and tail markings.

Voice: The male has a loud, drawling, nasal 'tzwee' which is very noticeable and often forms part of its twittering song.

Food: Larger seeds from trees, shrubs and weeds. Greenfinches have learnt to hang on nut bags to take peanuts.

Behaviour: Often surprisingly tame in gardens in winter. Visits nutbags. In spring, the male's song is not easy to miss, and the bird will usually be seen sitting in full view or flying slowly, with exaggerated deep wing beats, among the treetops, as part of its courtship display.

Breeding: The nest is placed in the fork of a tall shrub or tree. Often several pairs nest in a loose colony. There are 4-6 eggs and up to three broods in a nesting season.

LINNET

Carduelis cannabina

Habitat: Open land with abundant weeds, such as commons and heaths, young plantations and derelict industrial sites. Now rare on farmland. Prefers neglected gardens!

Distribution: Throughout Britain and Ireland but in north and west Scotland only as a migrant.

Seasons: Present all year round in most areas but some breeding birds winter in southern Europe and some northern European birds winter in Britain and Ireland.

Description: *Size* 13cm (5in). In breeding plumage males have a brilliant scarlet breast patch and, less noticeably, a scarlet forehead. These bright colours are lost in winter. Females and young are more uniformly brown, with speckled underparts. At all seasons, Linnets have a black and white strip along the edge of the closed wing and in flight show big white 'flashes' on the outer wing plus a contrasting white base and black tip to the tail.

Voice: Flight call a prolonged twitter. Song a fairly musical twitter of fluty and sharp notes. Flight calls and song are less liquid than those of Goldfinch.

Food: Seeds of small annual weeds such as groundsel, and insects.

Behaviour: Often in groups, concentrating where abundant weeds are seeding and feeding on them or the ground beneath. Flight low and bouncing with the Linnets calling continuously while in flight.

Breeding: Nest sited in dense low cover or on the ground. Gorse thickets sometimes contain colonies of the birds. Four to six eggs are laid and there may be up to three broods.

SISKIN

Carduelis spinus

Habitat: Coniferous woodland all year but also in birch and alder woods in winter, when gardens are sometimes visited.

Distribution: Breeds in the uplands of Scotland, northern England and Wales, and locally in the lowlands of southern England and Ireland where there are extensive coniferous woods. Outside the breeding season it is typically seen in birch and alder woods.

Seasons: Resident all year in breeding areas and with an influx of continental birds from September to May.

Description: *Size* 13cm (5in), noticeably smaller than a sparrow. The male is a brilliant yellow-green and black – much brighter than a Greenfinch. Females are duller than males, olive green above and pale yellow below, and young birds are duller still, being brownish and pale yellow, but both, like the male, have a double yellow wingbar on a blackish wing.

Voice: Two calls, a carrying, squeaky 'tsy-zi' and a wheezing 'tsu-weet'. The song is a rapid musical twitter ending in a drawn out wheezing discord.

Food: Mainly tree seeds.

Behaviour: A bird of the treetops where it is as acrobatic as a tit, swinging upside-down to feed on fir and alder cones, and on birch catkins. Outside the breeding season it usually occurs in flocks, often with Redpolls which are a closely related finch, heavily speckled brown above and more palely below, with red foreheads. In some areas Siskins regularly visit nutbags.

Breeding: Nests are built high in conifers with up to two broods of four or five being reared.

DUNNOCK

Prunella modularis

Habitat: The key requirement is low shrub cover and short vegetation at ground level or bare soil, so Dunnocks are found in most woodlands, hedges and gardens. Trees are not necessary.

Distribution: Almost all of Britain and Ireland.

Seasons: Resident in the same localities all year round.

Description: *Size* 14cm (5½in). At first glance a drab little bird, easily mistaken for a sparrow (and often called the Hedge Sparrow). Closer inspection reveals a distinctive blue-grey head and underparts and a slender beak unlike the stout bill of the sparrows. Both sexes look the same. Young Dunnocks have speckled underparts and are greyer than their parents. With both adults and young, their behaviour is a good means of identification.

Voice: A rapid warbling jingle, rather squeaky, with no really distinctive character: not as loud or rapid as a Wren's song and without the Robin's rather melancholy quality. The Dunnock's call is a high pitched 'tseep'.

Food: Small insects and seeds.

Behaviour: Dunnocks spend much time on the ground, adopting a crouching posture (unlike sparrows and robins) which makes them seem mouse-like as they creep around searching for food. Males often sing from low perches.

Breeding: The small nest, containing 4–5 bright blue eggs is placed in the low cover of a hedge or shrub or, sometimes, even in bundles of pea sticks or soft fruit bushes. Two or three broods may be reared.

Passer domesticus

Habitat: Lives very much in association with man in towns, villages and farm buildings. Ventures out to farmland in autumn to feed on ripening cereals' and stubbles.

Distribution: Almost all of Britain and Ireland but not uninhabited uplands. Introduced to and now common throughout the U.S.A. and southern Canada.

Seasons: Resident in its habitat throughout the year.

Description: *Size* 15cm (6in). Worth learning to identify properly, so as to avoid misidentifying other small brown birds as 'just sparrows'. Males always have grey crowns, with a small black bib in winter and a larger one in spring. Females and juveniles have buff heads and cheeks, speckled buff backs and pale underparts. In towns, individuals may become very dirty. Typically, House Sparrows appear dumpy birds with short legs, though they sometimes stand erect.

Voice: A chirp 'chee-ep' which can become a babble of noise when birds are squabbling or alarmed.

Food: Seeds and all sorts of domestic scraps, especially if based on cereals, such as bread and cake. Insects are important when rearing the young.

Behaviour: Gregarious, often nesting and feeding colonially. Dependent on humans and only rarely seen far from habitation. Unlike most British birds other than game birds and poultry, it cleans the plumage by dust bathing, a habit retained from its origins in the arid Middle East.

Breeding: An untidily woven grass nest is built, usually in a cavity under roof tiles but sometimes in usurped House Martin nests. There may be 3–6 eggs and up to four broods.

NUTHATCH

Sitta europaea

Habitat: Old trees in broadleaved woodland, parks and large gardens.
Distribution: England excluding the Isle of Wight, fenland and parts of the north. Wales excluding Anglesey. Not Scotland or Ireland.
Seasons: Resident.
Description: *Size* 14cm (5½in). In appearance it resembles a small woodpecker with a chisel beak, stumpy tail and short legs. Depending on the bird's position in a tree you may see only the blue-grey back or only the underparts. Adult males are quite reddish-brown on the flanks but females and juveniles are much paler.
Voice: A clear carrying 'ch-wit, ch-wit' often repeated. The song is a rapidly repeated 'chwee . . . chwee' a bit like a whistle with a big pea in it!
Food: Insects and spiders gathered from bark and foliage, tree seeds and nuts.
Behaviour: Usually seen clinging to the bark of the trunk or larger limbs of a big tree, where the bird climbs up or – the only British bird so skilled – comes downwards head first with equal ease. Sometimes feeds on the ground. Often detected by its call or by the hammering sound as it opens a carefully wedged nut with its powerful beak. In winter sometimes seen in flocks with tits. Occasionally visits birdtables and nutbags.
Breeding: Nests in holes which it plasters round with mud to exactly its own diameter, so excluding some competitors for nest sites, and predators. Up to nine eggs are laid and one brood is normal.

Motacilla alba

Habitat: The margins of lakes, ponds, streams and other waterbodies in lowlands and uplands. Farmland with livestock. Areas with short-mown grass including parks and gardens, and other open surfaces such as roads and car parks.

Distribution: All the British Isles.

Seasons: Resident but many move south in winter.

Description: *Size* 18cm (7in) including the long tail. Easily recognized by the combination of small size, pied plumage and ground-feeding habits. On young birds, grey-brown replaces the black colouring of head, back and wings.

Voice: The call is a loud cheerful 'chizzick', often repeated, and drawing attention to a bird flying overhead. The song is a twittering mix of calls.

Food: Insects picked from the ground or caught by jumping into the air.

Behaviour: Runs busily as it feeds on open ground or water margins. Constantly wags the long tail. Often seen in flight which is rapid and bounding. In winter roosts gregariously, sometimes seeking warm or sheltered sites such as greenhouses or ledges in cities. May feed on dropped fragments beneath birdtables, but more often forages on well-clipped lawns.

Breeding: The nest is placed in a cavity, commonly in drystone walls but also in piles of wood, outbuildings, holes in the ground or behind thatch or creepers. Open-fronted nestboxes are also used. Usually there are 5–6 eggs and up to three broods.

STARLING

Sturnus vulgaris

Habitat: Mature broadleaved and conifer woodland, hedgerow and park trees, farmland and gardens.

Distribution: Throughout the British Isles. Introduced to and now common throughout the U.S.A. and southern Canada.

Seasons: British birds are resident but great numbers come to Britain in October from northern and north-eastern Europe until spring.

Description: *Size* 21cm (8in). In winter, both sexes have their plumage spangled with white spots. These disappear entirely from the male in spring when it acquires an iridescent green-purple sheen. The female retains a few spots all summer. Young birds are grey-brown overall with a whitish throat, eventually gaining the spotty winter plumage of the parents. Young birds slightly resemble young Blackbirds but much shorter tailed, more erect and walk or run rather than hopping as Blackbirds do.

Voice: A harsh 'tscheer' and a whistle 'tsee-oo', both descending in scale. The song is a medley of whistles and gurgles with much mimicry of other birds' calls often also including human whistles and telephone noises.

Food: Worms, leatherjackets and other soil insects, seeds and berries, fruit, cereals and domestic scraps.

Behaviour: The relatively upright stance and waddling walk are very characteristic. Frequently in parties or flocks, sometimes feeding on farmland with Rooks and Jackdaws. Massive winter roosts of Starlings form in city centres where warmth and shelter are greater than in rural areas.

Breeding: The nest is placed in a hole in a tree, quarry or building. There can be two broods of up to seven.

Certhia familiaris

Habitat: Woodlands, especially those with mature trees. Trees in hedges, parks and gardens particularly if close to woods.

Distribution: Throughout the British Isles but absent from the northern and western isles.

Seasons: Resident.

Description: *Size* 13cm (5in). A little mouse-like bird, speckled brown above and white below, with a long curved beak designed for probing in crannies in bark. The tail is short and used as a support in climbing. Adults and juveniles have rather similar plumages.

Voice: A thin, high-pitched 'tsee' call. The song is easily missed – a weak squeaky 'tsee-tsee-tsee-tsissi-tsee', more like an insect than a bird.

Food: Insects and spiders found on or in the cracks of bark.

Behaviour: Quite unmistakable. Treecreepers feed by climbing steadily up the trunk or larger boughs of a tree and then fly down to start again on another one. Very rarely seen away from woods but will visit adjoining gardens especially if they contain large, rough-barked trees. Sometimes the birds excavate fist-sized roosting cavities in the soft bark of old redwood trees. Not particularly shy but easily overlooked as they are unobtrusive and well camouflaged. Sometimes joins tit flocks in winter.

Breeding: The nest is made behind a flap of loose bark or behind ivy at any height up to 10m (about 33ft). There are sometimes two broods of five or six young.

WAXWING

Bombycilla garrulus

Habitat: Hedges and scrub, parks and gardens.

Distribution: Largely eastern Scotland and north-east England. More rarely, the Midlands and East Anglia. Can occur further south and west into Wales and Ireland. It breeds in north-west America and winters erratically in central and western U.S.A.

Seasons: A winter visitor, usually in very small numbers but about once a decade more abundant. Rarely arrives in Britain and Ireland before November and may be present until April. Numbers which arrive depend on whether there has been a warm summer and good winter in the previous year, causing a population build-up, followed by failure of the continental berry crop, especially rowan, that winter. In such years, several thousand may reach the British Isles.

Description: *Size* 18cm (7in), slightly smaller than a Starling. The chubby appearance accentuated by the thick neck and short tail, plus the crest, waxy red markings on the wings and yellow markings on both wings and tail, make it quite unmistakable.

Voice: The call is a weak, high trilling 'zhree'.

Food: In winter mainly berries. Arriving after Fieldfares and Red-wings have taken their toll of rowan, hawthorn and holly, Waxwings are often forced to feed on berry-bearing shrubs in gardens and unpicked fruit in orchards. In mild spells they may fly catch, at which they are adept – their summer diet is mosquitoes.

Behaviour: Acrobatic when feeding on slender boughs and twigs. Very rarely seen singly. Flocks may be only a few birds or, exceptionally, hundreds strong.

Troglodytes troglodytes

Habitat: Low cover in woodland, thickets and bracken, hedgerows, stream sides, parks and gardens.

Distribution: Throughout the British Isles. Very abundant in suitable habitat. Resident western seaboard of America, summer visitor in southern Canada and north-east U.S.A., winter visitor in southern and eastern U.S.A. and is called the Winter Wren.

Seasons: Resident, plus some winter migrants from Continent.

Description: *Size* 10cm (4in). A dumpy, round brown little bird with a short tail always held vertically cocked. On close inspection the Wren is rather handsome with its pale eye-stripe, long slender beak and delicate barring on the flanks and rear.

Voice: Disproportionately loud. The call is an irritable ticking sometimes followed by a prolonged scolding 'churrr'. The song is an explosion of quick notes followed by a trill, repeated after brief pauses.

Food: Mainly insects and spiders found in low growth or on the ground.

Behaviour: Obtrusively noisy, singing loudly in spring and scolding humans. Normally seen briefly, slipping through cover in hedge bottom or shrubbery. The slender beak is used to probe crevices and, in winter especially, Wrens work systematically over fences or other structures where prey may be concealed. It often roosts communally in winter.

Breeding: Builds a domed nest with a tiny entrance hole, often placed in a cavity in a stump or in ivy and camouflaged with moss. The male builds several nests and the female selects one in which to lay 5–6 eggs. There can be two broods.

43

CUCKOO

Cuculus canorus

Habitat: Cuckoos use all sorts of habitats, from town parks to treeless uplands, and will visit gardens where song birds are nesting, to prospect for egg-laying opportunities.

Distribution: Throughout Britain and Ireland.

Seasons: Usually arriving by mid-April, the adults leave in July or August, with young birds following once they are fit to do so in September or October.

Description: *Size* 33cm (13in). Cuckoos have a very hawkish appearance, because of their slender build, long wings and tail, and barred underparts. Usually the females are grey like the males, but some have upperparts brown barred with black and pale underparts also heavily barred. Young birds may be similarly brown or dark grey-brown and have a noticeable white patch on the back of the head. Cuckoos often fly low with fast, shallow wingbeats.

Voice: The familiar 'cuck-oo' and a hoarse 'whow-whow-whow'. The female has a loud bubbling call.

Food: Mainly large caterpillars.

Behaviour: Tends to be shy and quick to fly off at human approach, but when two birds are engaged in courtship they may perch in the open and call noisily. It sometimes feeds on the ground.

Breeding: Eggs are laid singly in the nests of other birds. The most common hosts in gardens are Dunnocks, but many other species are parasitized including Robins, Wrens and Blackbirds. When it hatches, the young cuckoo ejects other eggs and chicks so that the hosts' whole efforts are devoted to its care.

Dendrocopus major

Habitat: Occurs in mature woodland of all types, hedgerows near woods, parks and gardens.

Distribution: As a breeding bird, Britain except the Isle of Man and the northern and western Isles of Scotland. Autumn migrants may occur anywhere in Britain and Ireland.

Seasons: Resident. Winter visitors from Scandinavia sometimes arrive in large numbers.

Description: *Size* 23cm (9in). A white blaze on the wings and red patch on the vent are obvious ways of distinguishing this bird from the Lesser Spotted Woodpecker which has a pattern of bars across the wings and back and completely pale underparts: the Lesser Spotted Woodpecker is also much smaller. Female Great Spotted Woodpeckers lack red on the back of the head. Juveniles have completely red crowns.

Voice: A short, mechanical sounding 'tchick', delivered in flight and at rest, which carries far and is usually the first clue to the bird's presence. The breeding 'song' is a remarkably loud drumming made by striking a resonating branch with the beak at machinegun speed in sudden bursts.

Food: Wood-boring insects extracted from rotting wood in trees, on the ground, nestlings, caterpillars collected from foliage. Seeds extracted from conifer cones and collected from the ground; berries.

Behaviour: Hard to see in trees where it is adept at hiding, but its loud call draws attention, especially when in deeply undulating flight. deeply undulating flight.

Breeding: Hole excavated in soft or rotting wood of tree trunk, low or high. There is one brood of 4–7 eggs.

SWIFT

Apus apus

Habitat: May be seen in flight anywhere, often at great altitude, but very largely dependent on buildings for nest sites.

Distribution: Breeds throughout the British Isles except for the west and extreme north of Scotland.

Seasons: The last summer migrant to arrive and the first to leave, Swifts appear in early to mid-May and depart again in mid-August, though a few stragglers may be seen in September.

Description: *Size* 17cm (6½in). The most noticeable aspect of a Swift is its scythe-like wings – very slender and curved back to the tips – which are flapped stiffly and very fast. By contrast, Swallows, House Martins and Sand Martins have shorter, broader wings and show pale underparts whereas the Swift has only a whitish chin which is barely noticeable.

Voice: A distinctive chattering scream.

Food: All sorts of small insects caught in flight.

Behaviour: Normally lives in colonies and occurs in flocks. 'Screaming parties' occur around nest sites, with groups of birds excitedly chasing each other at low altitude round church towers or between houses. Birds will hunt low over water or land, and rise to great heights. Mating takes place on the wing. Swifts never perch but will sometimes cling to the walls of buildings.

Breeding: The nest is built under cover in the roofs of buildings, or rarely in a cliff crevice, wherever there is an unobstructed approach, the birds needing to fly straight in and out. Two to three young may be reared.